Over 50? Start Your Business!

Brian D. Jones

www.TheMaturEntrepreneur.com

DEDICATION

To every person over 50 brave enough to start their business.

And to my wife, Carrie Regnolds Jones.

TABLE OF CONTENTS

ACKNOWLEDGMENTS

To Nick Loper for his valuable editing. To Ida Fia Sveningsson for her work on the book cover. To Chandler Bolt and the rest of the team at Self-Publishing School. To Megan Jamison for coaching me along. To Debbie and Steven Lum for keeping me accountable along the way. To Charles DiLisio for his friendship and photography skills. To Brian Hale for being a good friend and sounding board. And finally, to my wife Carrie Regnolds Jones, MD for joining me on this crazy ride

INTRODUCTION

You're concerned about your future. Maybe even a little scared.

Important practical questions keep coming to mind:

"Will I be able to take care of my family?"

"What happens if I lose my job?"

"How can I bring in more income?"

"Am I doing enough to build wealth?"

"Is my retirement nest egg big enough?"

Other, more personal questions also nag at you:

"Am I proud of what I'm doing?"

"Am I following my passion?"

"Do I control my destiny?"

"Am I truly using all my experience and skills?"

"Am I building a legacy?"

1

Then the light bulb goes on. The answer to all your questions.

You need to start your own business.

Starting and running your own successful business checks all the boxes.

Building wealth? Check.

Controlling your destiny? Check.

Leaving a legacy? Check.

You are psyched! Let's do this!

Then you hear that familiar voice in your head. You know it well. It keeps saying things like:

> *"You're too old."*

> *"You don't have any good business ideas."*

> *"No customer will buy from you."*

> *"You'll embarrass yourself."*

> *"You'll fail. Or you'll quit. So don't even start."*

Now you have an important choice.

You can listen to that voice in your head, stay the course, and keep doing what you're doing.

Or you can read this book.

Over 50? Start Your Business! is a step-by-step roadmap to build the future you want.

Specifically designed for Mature Entrepreneurs. Based on solid research and proven best practices. Leading you through the process of creating and starting your dream business – even if you have no business ideas right now.

The business landscape has changed dramatically in recent years. The world is more connected than ever. You know this. But what you don't know is that this Connected Economy offers tremendous new business opportunities for YOU. Opportunities that didn't even exist just a few years ago.

I'm going to show you these possibilities and how you can take advantage of them to achieve your goals.

Who am I to write this guide?

Well for one, I'm 57 years old at the time this is being published. And you can be sure I had that same voice in my head doubting my every move. [spoiler alert: that voice LIES]

For over 20 years I've been in business for myself. I learned what worked and what didn't. But I learned the hard way. There were a lot of wrong turns, dead ends, and far too much wasted time.

Today, you have the distinct advantage of learning from my mistakes so you don't have to repeat them. In fact, I've been sharing important lessons on my site, TheMaturEntrepreneur.com.

Too many entrepreneurial books are written for the younger set who have a completely different perspective when starting a business. My Mission is to inspire and support Mature Entrepreneurs. (In the book, you'll learn how to discover your own Mission.)

I've boiled down these ideas into an easy to follow, step-by-step guide for those over 50 starting their business today.

This is the book I wish already existed. A book I would want to read. A book for those over 50 who want to start their dream business.

In short, I wrote this book for YOU.

I want you to start YOUR dream business. A business that's perfect for you, whether it's a full-time startup or a part-time lifestyle business.

A business that gives you financial security, aligns with your passion, and builds your legacy.

I have a secret to share. You are not the only person over 50 who dreams of starting a new business. I'd even dare to say a wave is forming.

According to research by the Kauffman Foundation, founders over 50 years old are the fastest growing segment of new company founders. Nesta Foundation research has found that companies founded by older people are also much more likely to be successful. And these findings don't even include all the people over 50 doing side businesses.

You are in good company. You may even have friends or colleagues who have started businesses. One acquaintance of mine who retired as an engineer now has a thriving business selling premium tea. Another friend transitioned out of her successful corporate career and now markets her own line of women's equestrian clothing.

The possibilities are only limited by your imagination.

Follow the guidance of this book, and like magic, your perfect business will reveal itself.

Now is the time to read this book. Now is the time to begin. Now is the time to start your perfect business.

Or you can wait. Think it over. Decide later. (It's that voice again!)

But time keeps on ticking, and we've got a limited number of heartbeats left.

It's up to you.

Begin reading this book right now. You will learn so much about yourself. You will create a new way of life better than you could have ever imagined.

You WILL start your dream business.

It's time to build wealth. Time to take control of your destiny. Time to leave a legacy.

CHAPTER 1 – THE PATH TO YOUR DREAM BUSINESS

I'm so pleased you've made it to the first chapter of the book! You've crossed the threshold. You've chosen yourself. You're on your way to starting your dream business.

Remember why you've come this far. You want financial security. You want to control your destiny. You want to leave a legacy.

This chapter maps the journey you are about to take. It's the top-level view so that you can see how everything fits together. I've created the graphic that follows to guide you. You can download a copy of this graphic on my website in the book resources area.

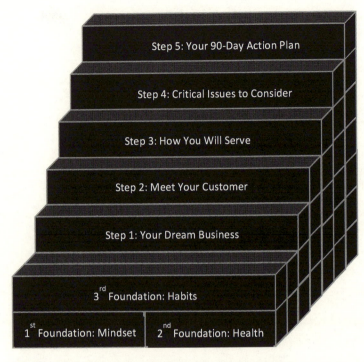

Step 5: Your 90-Day Action Plan

Step 4: Critical Issues to Consider

Step 3: How You Will Serve

Step 2: Meet Your Customer

Step 1: Your Dream Business

3rd Foundation: Habits

1st Foundation: Mindset   2nd Foundation: Health

Notice that your journey has two major parts:

- The **3 Foundations** for Success.
- The **5 Steps** to Starting Your Dream Business.

The 3 Foundations are the base required to make your journey a success. These are the same foundations I've seen used by nearly all successful entrepreneurs, and the foundations I created for myself.

The 3 Foundations are Mindset, Health, and Habits. You may already have one or more of these foundations in place. But you must constantly strengthen these foundations to succeed when over 50.

The next three chapters focus on these foundations.

Chapter 2 introduces you to Mindset. Starting a business over 50 requires a completely new Mindset. I will show you some surprising research on Mindset, and what it means for Mature Entrepreneurs. I will share with you best practices in building the proper Mindset, including the ones I use myself.

Chapter 3 covers the important foundation of Health. I won't sugarcoat it; starting a business is challenging. Top entrepreneurs of all ages make Health a focus, or they don't last long. This is doubly important if you are over 50. We'll cover the case for Health, the major elements of your personal health, and what you need to do to get healthy to face the challenges – and reap the rewards – of starting your business.

The focus of **Chapter 4** is the foundation of Habits. This is a critical foundation because developing the right habits makes everything possible. Starting a business requires good habits. Habits make living your life easier and more enjoyable, and keep you going when the going gets tough. I will share research on Habits and provide best practices on Habits you'll want to consider adding to your own toolkit.

The foundations actually come with a powerful bonus. They'll serve you in everything you do, not just in starting your business.

My life was immeasurably improved by building the foundations I will share with you. I was shocked at how dramatic the improvement was. I can say without hesitation that this book would not exist without my foundations.

Chapter 5 begins the steps to starting your dream business. In Step 1, we begin by defining your dream business. In this step, you get to create your perfect future. It's fun! You get to explore your passions and the things that get you most excited. One of the secrets of the Connected Economy is that your passion can be your business. It's no longer one or the other.

Chapter 6 gives you the second step toward your dream business. In Step 2, you get to meet your customers. You'll learn how to find loyal customers who are just as excited about your passions as you are. This is one of the most dramatic changes in the

Connected Economy. Successful businesses take full advantage of this, and you will learn to do it too.

Chapter 7 details the third step toward your dream business. In Step 3, you will discover how you will serve your customers. You will build on what you've learned about yourself and what you've learned about your customers. You will uncover ideal products and services your customers want and that you will be excited to provide.

Chapter 8 covers the fourth step of the process. Where you consider critical issues in service of your customers. In Step 4, you will take an inventory of your unique combination of experience and skills. I stress the word "unique" because nobody in the world has your exact mix. You will fully understand what YOU can offer your customers.

Chapter 9 puts into motion all your hard work up to that point in the fifth and final step. In Step 5, you create your 90-Day Action Plan to get things off the ground and bring your dream business to life.

This plan will guide you every day and serve as your marching orders.

Your Action Plan will keep you moving forward during those critical first 90 days. If you follow your plan, you'll be doing the right things at the right times and building unstoppable momentum.

Here's our roadmap:

1. Build The **3 Foundations**.
2. Follow The **5 Steps**.
3. **Start** your dream business.

Let's get started. There's no time to waste—you're not getting any younger.

On to the first foundation: The Success Mindset.

CHAPTER 2 – THE FIRST FOUNDATION: MINDSET

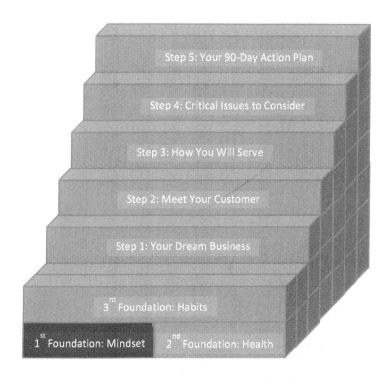

Step 5: Your 90-Day Action Plan

Step 4: Critical Issues to Consider

Step 3: How You Will Serve

Step 2: Meet Your Customer

Step 1: Your Dream Business

3rd Foundation: Habits

1st Foundation: Mindset

2nd Foundation: Health

In this chapter, you start building your first foundation: The Success Mindset to Start Your Business.

Your dreams will only come true when you "Get Your Mind Right." This chapter will help you do just that.

The first step is to *convince* your mind why starting your business is a smart move.

You'll say to yourself "Yes, I must DO this!"

But your mind also tries to talk you out of your dreams. You'll learn why this happens and what you can do to counter your negative self-talk.

Finally, I'll share some "pearls of wisdom" that myself and others have found helpful and inspirational in creating a Success Mindset.

Ready to get into your head?

THE CASE FOR STARTING YOUR BUSINESS WHILE OVER 50

Let's start with a couple of brief history lessons.

Lesson 1: People Who Started a Business After Age 50

Joseph Campbell – started Campbell's Soup at age 52

Ray Kroc – started McDonald's at age 52

Arianna Huffington – started the Huffington Post at age 54

Estée Lauder – founded Estée Lauder at age 54

Ferdinand Porsche – founded Porsche at age 56

Kawasaki Shozo – founded Kawasaki Heavy Industries at age 59

Amadeo Giannini – founded Bank of America at age 60

Charles Flint – started IBM at age 61

Wally Blume – started Denali Flavors at age 62

Col. Harlan Sanders – started KFC at age 65

Jeanne Dowell – co-founded Green Buddha clothing at age 80

Lesson 2: People Who Enjoyed Their First Success After Age 50

Raymond Chandler – first novel was published at age 51

Julia Child – began her PBS cooking show at age 51

Kathryn Joosten – Emmy winner started her acting career at age 56

Frank McCourt – Pulitzer Prize winner started writing at age 64

Oscar Swahn – won Olympic gold at age 64, Olympic silver at age 72

Laura Ingalls Wilder – published her first novel at age 65

Peter Mark Roget – published the first Roget's Thesaurus at age 70

Harriet Doerr – National Book Award winner was first published at age 74

Norman Maclean – published his only novel *A River Runs Through It* at age 74

Grandma Moses – painted her first canvas at age 76

These examples make it clear that age is no barrier to starting a business or enjoying success later in life. And think of the thousands of others over 50 who were successful on a smaller scale without the fame.

So, yes you CAN do this!

THE NEW SCIENCE OF AGING

Science provides the next argument for starting your business. I want to focus on two critical findings: The Promise of Longevity and The Miracle of Neuroplasticity.

The Promise of Longevity

Life expectancy is increasing. If you are 50 years old today, you can expect to live another 30 years or more. This brings up two issues. The first issue is having enough money to live comfortably for the rest of your long life. The second issue is how you spend that time. What do you hope to accomplish with the remainder of your one and only life?

Starting a business is a great way to address both issues. A successful business will generate income, build wealth, and serve others. You will be in control of your own destiny and legacy.

The Miracle of Neuroplasticity

There's an old saying: "You can't teach an old dog new tricks."

It turns out that saying is WRONG.

Common knowledge in the past was that our brains peaked in our early 20s, and it was all downhill after that. Prevailing wisdom was that nothing could be done to increase the brain's capacity as we aged; slowing the decline was our only hope.

As a person with a lifelong love of learning, this "accepted fact" always bothered me. I hoped to be an exception to that rule.

It turns out that EVERYONE is the exception to that rule.

Within the last twenty years, technologies such as functional magnetic resonance imaging (fMRI) have debunked the old-dog-new-tricks myth. Scientists have found that the brain can grow and make new connections at any age. The scientific term for this is neuroplasticity.

The implications are profound.

We don't have to passively accept inevitable mental decline as we age. We can grow and build new neural connections throughout our adult life.

In fact, doing so is actually beneficial to our health and well-being.

It is best to challenge ourselves mentally, to "stretch" our brains. You have the capacity to learn and do things you've always wanted to do but thought were no longer within your grasp.

Starting a business is just such a challenge. It can be done at any age, and this challenge comes with the unique rewards of serving others, creating wealth, and building a legacy.

THE CONNECTED ECONOMY

We now live in a Connected World, characterized by instant access to information and virtually limitless global connections.

A major part of this new Connected World is the Connected Economy.

Those of us over 50 weren't born into this Connected Economy like our younger counterparts, but we can still take full advantage of it. Along with these exciting changes come both challenges and opportunities.

Challenges of the Connected Economy

We all remember when many blue-collar jobs were eliminated a couple of decades ago. This was devastating to the individuals and families involved. The culprit was outsourcing and globalization.

The same thing is happening now to white-collar jobs.

I won't sugarcoat it.

Job security is a myth. No job is safe. The Financial Crisis of 2008 showed this all too well. So-called "knowledge jobs" – jobs that were thought to be safe just a generation ago – are on the chopping block.

The downside of the Connected Economy is that it allows the potential for any job to be eliminated. This happens through a combination of two things: technology investments that replace labor, and the ease of outsourcing knowledge work to an educated overseas workforce.

And who has the bulls-eye on their back?

YOU, the over-50-worker whose salary is higher than that of younger workers.

YOU, the over-50-worker whose experience and skills aren't valued by your employer.

Cuts ARE coming in the next economic downturn, if not sooner.

How secure do you feel about your eventual retirement?

Given the status of Social Security. Given the status of pensions. Given health care system costs. Given your investments.

Given the promise of longevity.

Starting your business gives you a chance to create wealth. A chance to provide security. A chance to control your destiny. A chance to create your legacy. And most importantly, a chance to serve others.

Opportunities in the Connected Economy

I'll let you in on a secret.

This secret took me years of research and personal experience to learn, and it's one that very few of my over-50 peers understand.

Here's the secret:

Despite the scary downsides, the Connected Economy is the single greatest economic opportunity in history!

It's that big!

People are following their dreams in the Connected Economy. People are creating their perfect business in the Connected Economy.

I'm creating MY perfect business in the Connected Economy. This book is part of my business. This book exists because of the Connected Economy. Ten years ago, the thought of publishing a book myself and launching to an audience of millions would have been absurd.

The Connected Economy allows these opportunities to happen, and makes creating your dream business easier than you can imagine.

But you need a different Mindset. A Mindset of Success. A Mindset of Growth. A Mindset of Wealth, in every sense of the word.

And the good news is we can have any Mindset we want. Bodies of scientific evidence support this – that Mindset is a choice.

YOUR SUCCESS MINDSET

I've spent a significant amount of time exploring the Mindset of Success, and I've found certain characteristics that appear time and time again.

Don't be overwhelmed by what follows. Read them quickly. Decide which ones make sense to you.

Now is the time for introduction, not mastery. Don't expect to pick up these characteristics all at once. Instead, plan to return later when you create your own personal Success Mindset.

One characteristic of a Success Mindset is **a positive attitude.**

It sounds simple, but it is difficult to put into practice. After all, as mammals, our survival depends on recognizing dangers. We're biologically programmed to be on alert for risks and negatives, because self-preservation is a top priority and that lion might eat us! And even though lion attacks are exceedingly rare in our modern concrete and corporate jungles, we still focus on the negative. Just go to your favorite news source and read the headlines. The headlines that grab your attention are almost all negative.

Research in the newer field of positive psychology found that we need at least three positive messages to counter a single negative message. No wonder it is so difficult to have a positive attitude!

The science on mindset has found two things to be helpful in cultivating and maintaining a positive attitude.

The first is to **play to your strengths.** We all have unique character strengths, and if you haven't taken inventory lately of what yours may be, I recommend taking the time to do so.

One resource for this is AuthenticHappiness.org, where you can take the free VIA Survey of Character Strengths. After you take the survey, they give you a personal ranking of your character strengths in 24 different areas.

When I did the survey, my two top character strengths happen to be Love of Learning and Curiosity. I think it's fair to say this book is the direct result of what I've been curious to learn!

The second part of a positive attitude is being **grateful.** I like the phrase "an attitude of gratitude."

You have to work at gratitude. One common technique is a keep a gratitude journal. Every day just write down at least three things for which you are grateful. Family, friends, the fact you are alive, all are possibilities.

As I wake up, I like to spend a few moments thinking about things for which I am grateful.

I am grateful you are reading this book.

A MINDSET OF SERVICE

A Success Mindset is a mindset of service. Here are a few characteristics of a Service Mindset.

An Outward Focus

Those with a Service Mindset look outside themselves. Their focus is on those they wish to serve. Wharton professor Adam Grant's research identifies people as either givers, takers, or matchers. Givers try to better others. Takers try to get the most they can out of others. Matchers act as givers toward givers, and act as takers toward other takers.

Be a giver. Surround yourself with other givers and matchers. Avoid takers.

A Desire for Significance

Those with a Service Mindset have a desire to do something significant for those they wish to serve. They measure success by the positive impact they have.

No Personal Expectations

Those with a Service Mindset have no expectations for themselves. They understand that when things become better for those they serve good things will come to them too.

A MINDSET OF GROWTH

Carol Dweck has done significant research on mindset. In fact, she's even written a bestselling book on the topic, called *Mindset*. She found that people fall into two groups.

One group has what she labeled a Fixed Mindset. Those with a Fixed Mindset feel that their lives and brain capacity are static. Fixed Mindset people believe they can't change, get better, or grow. As you might expect, these people tend to give up easily when the going gets tough.

In contrast, Dweck found that all successful people have a Growth Mindset. Those with a Growth Mindset feel that they can learn and grow. They accept and fight through the challenges they face. More importantly, they believe this is true for others as well.

The best leaders have a Growth Mindset. They give others credit when things go well, and take the blame when things go poorly.

I spent much of my life in a Fixed Mindset. This often happens to people who enjoy success at a young age. But my challenges and struggles eventually came, and with a Fixed Mindset, I was poorly equipped to meet those challenges. I had to adopt Growth Mindset to overcome them.

And that's the good news; you get to choose which Mindset will be your "operating system."

A SENSE OF URGENCY

Another Success Mindset characteristic is a sense of urgency. Don't let opportunity pass you by. Being over 50, you already have a built-in sense of urgency.

AN ACTION BIAS

Don't wait. A bias for action does not mean being reckless. Successful people pick their best direction. They then do what's needed to move forward. Action builds momentum. Be confident the details will work themselves out along the way.

Don't Listen to the Negatives

To meet any challenge, you first have to talk yourself into doing it.

I already mentioned that we are hard-wired to see the negative; it's an evolutionary risk aversion. That same trait also makes us hesitant to change when we are not in immediate danger.

This appears in what I call the Voice of Judgment (VOJ).

The VOJ wants the status quo. That's when the VOJ is happy. It's that voice in your head criticizing everything you dream to do.

The VOJ says you're not good enough. That you shouldn't try because you'll fail.

The VOJ says you're too OLD to start a business in the Connected Economy.

Here's what I have learned.

The VOJ in your head is NOT you. It's just a voice that thinks it's protecting you. Don't listen to your VOJ. It lies.

The VOJ has subtler ways to keep you from achieving your dreams as well. I call them the "Unwanted P's":

- Perfectionism
- Procrastination
- Paralysis

Good is better than perfect.

Don't wait. Just do it.

Ready, Fire, Aim.

Thankfully, there's another voice inside you too: your own voice of wisdom. This is the voice of your "gut feelings."

Listen to your gut instead. I do.

You'll encounter other negative voices on your entrepreneurial path as well. These are real voices. These are the voices of your doubters and haters.

Worse, some doubters will be people you trust, family and friends. They will try to talk you out of your dreams. They will give you a laundry list of reasons why you shouldn't go for it.

Don't listen to them.

They *believe* that they are looking out for your best interests, helping you avoid failure and embarrassment.

But here's what's really going on.

When you follow your dreams, you WILL change. You will change for the better.

They know that. And they know that when you change, their relationship with you will have to change. They don't want to deal with change. They may not want to face that they should change themselves.

Follow your dreams. Lead by example.

The other doubters are the "so-called" experts. Pundits who make blanket statements about "you" without even knowing YOU. "Over 50 is too old to start a business. Leave that to the younger generation."

Ignore them.

Then there are the haters. When you follow your dreams in the Connected Economy, the haters will come out of the woodwork. They are the trolls. They have nothing better to do than to attack your dreams, because they don't have dreams themselves.

Feel compassion for them, but ignore them. Do not respond. Just do your work.

In the Connected Economy, everything you do is out there for all to see. That is a good thing when you follow your dreams. Here is the reaction you must expect:

- 1/3 will love what you are doing (your fans)
- 1/3 will hate what you are doing (your haters)
- 1/3 won't care

When you follow your dreams, do it for yourself and for your fans.

Ignore your haters.

PEARLS OF WISDOM

I'd like to close this chapter on Mindset with a few pearls of wisdom that have been valuable for me.

Take 100% Responsibility for Your Life

Everything changed for me when I read this principle in Jack Canfield's *The Success Principles*. Anything is possible when you fully accept responsibility for your life. Be realistic. You gain control when you take responsibility. My life took a 180-degree turn for the better.

The Golden Rule

Treat others the way you wish to be treated. Demand this same treatment from others.

The Serenity Prayer

...Grant me the Serenity

To accept the things I cannot change

Courage to change the things I can

And wisdom to know the difference.

Letting Go

Focus on your own efforts. You can't control the results.

Progress, Not Perfection

Keep moving forward toward your dreams. Change doesn't happen all at once.

Limiting Beliefs

Everyone has limiting beliefs. These are just BELIEFS—not truths. Replace these limiting beliefs with what Mature Entrepreneur Michael Hyatt calls "enabling truths."

Being Authentic

Authenticity is valuable in the Connected Economy. YOUR true story is all you can tell. People will know if you are not genuine. When you are authentic, you will attract the right people. I like the following quote by Jim Rohn: *"Success is something you attract by the person you become."*

Get Out of Your Comfort Zone

Building a business will require getting outside of your comfort zone. It will make you uneasy and it will be a challenge, but you can't fly if you never leave the nest.

Your Five

Jim Rohn also says: *"You are the average of the five people you spent the most time with."* Look around. Are your closest peers and confidants on the same mission as you? Do they support your dreams? Remember, in the Connected Economy, your "five" can be located anywhere.

Help with Your Success Mindset

In the Connected Economy, there are several ways others can help you nurture your Success Mindset:

- Meetup groups
- Accountability partners
- Mentors

- Virtual mentors you learn from who don't know you

- Mastermind groups

- Coaches

The final two pearls of wisdom are the most important when starting a business. I want to introduce them to you here.

What is your WHY?

This is THE most important question you must ask yourself as you start your business. WHY do you want to do this? Everything flows from your WHY. We will revisit your WHY in the first step.

Create a Vision and Mission Statement

A Vision Statement takes your WHY and creates a destination for you. A Mission Statement says how you will get there.

I'll share in detail how to write these in Step 3 later. These are primary activities as you define your dream business.

We covered a lot in this chapter. The Mindset foundation is critical.

We stated the case for starting your business while over the age of 50.

You learned the characteristics of your Success Mindset to make it happen.

You were introduced to negative self-talk and how to counter it.

Finally, you learned "pearls of wisdom" to keep your Success Mindset strong, including the importance of knowing your WHY and the introduction of Vision and Mission Statements to focus your efforts.

Now it's time to add the second foundation: your health.

CHAPTER 3 – THE SECOND FOUNDATION: HEALTH

In this chapter, you'll start building your second foundation: your health

Starting your business will be challenging. There will be good times and there will be tough times, but through it all you must take care of your health. This is critical both for your own well-being and for those you wish to serve.

Health has three components:

1. Physical health
2. Mental health
3. Spiritual health

PHYSICAL HEALTH

Being over 50, you may already obsess about your health. I'm probably guilty of that! Or maybe you sweep thinking about your health under the rug, hoping the issue will go away.

One thing is certain: without physical health, achieving your dreams will be difficult. Improving your physical health starts with knowing your baseline health status from which you can maintain or improve. Next, you need to address the fundamental elements of your physical health; nutrition, fitness, and sleep.

See Your Doctor

Seeing your doctor is the first step. Hopefully you already see your doctor on a regular basis. You need to know where you stand today to get an understanding of your health baseline. This is your jumping off point for better health.

During your visit, medications can be made up to date and any serious issues can be found and addressed immediately.

Doctor visits are tough for me. I don't like them at all. You see, I'm a fainter. Several times I have passed out when giving blood. Even doing the small finger pricks. The blood bank actually told me never to come back again!

But I force myself to see my doctor and I'm fortunate to be in good health. On my last visit, my doctor said, "Keep doing what you're doing." I want my next visit to be even better.

Nutrition

Nutrition is critical for health. Here's the most important thing you must understand about nutrition:

You are what you eat.

Good food nourishes you. Poor food is empty calories.

Good food is medicine. Poor food is poison.

The current food system is out of whack. The industrial food system was created to produce lots of food cheaply, and it does that very well. But it is making us sick. Many things you buy at the grocery store are created in food laboratories. These products are engineered to artificially improve taste, increase shelf life, and maximize profits. Most of these foods are highly processed, and stripped of nutritional value.

It's a broken system. But you can choose NOT to be part of that system. I did, and it has made all the difference.

Starting with grocery shopping, I learned to "shop the edges." Grocery stores are designed so that the fresh foods are generally found around the edge of the store. The center of the store is where you find all the processed foods to avoid. Make sure most of your purchases come from the edges of the grocery store.

Another good choice is to shop at local farmer's markets. There you will find fresh locally-grown fruits, vegetables, and other items produced by the people selling them.

A growing option is to join a Community Supported Agriculture (CSA) program. When you join a CSA, you become a part owner of what is grown each season on a specific farm. Periodically you receive a box of the best that farm has to offer. You get to try new things, and enjoy produce that was freshly picked at the peak of its ripeness and nutritional value.

How I Eat

My nutrition was the first thing I did to take 100% responsibility for my life.

I had been overweight most of my adult life as a result of eating the Standard American Diet (SAD). I was constantly trying one diet or another; high protein, high carb, high fat... you name it, I've tried it.

In February 2015, I made the commitment to eating healthy nutritious food in controlled (but not small) portions. These meals were nutrient-dense but not calorie-dense.

Here are my day-to-day food choices:

- Small servings of animal protein, at most once per day.

- The bulk of my protein and my carbohydrates come from "slow carbs" – beans, legumes, and whole grains.

- At least six servings of vegetables.

- At least five servings of fruits.

- A couple of daily handfuls of nuts/seeds.

- Water and tea only to drink.

Since I am a human, I also have occasional "Free Days" when I eat what I feel like eating. But I always return to the day-to-day food choices.

As a result, I feel great.

I've dropped about one pound per week in the 7 months I've been eating like this, and the crazier thing is I'm now actually consuming 50% *more* calories per day than I was before I made this dietary shift. The shift to nutritionally dense calories has made all the difference. Honestly, I can say that I feel better now than in the past 25 years.

Exercise

Another component of physical health is regular exercise. Put simply, our bodies were built to move.

Unfortunately, too many people over 50 don't have enough physical activity. I hope you are not one of those people.

Starting your business requires stamina and focus. Regular exercise will keep you at your best. There's a reason Sir Richard Branson (age 65) says exercise is his #1 productivity hack.

Walking and resistance training are at the core of my fitness program. I typically lift weights three days per week. I take a long power walk twice per week. And I try to incorporate walking into activities on the weekends.

Walking is your best choice if just beginning. A good pair of walking shoes is all that is required. Walking gets you outdoors. You can walk on a path, around your neighborhood, or even in a mall during bad weather. You can walk a comfortable distance at a comfortable pace. And build your distance and speed over time.

Resistance training is a necessary part of fitness over 50. We lose muscle mass over time unless we do regular resistance training.

Resistance training can be as simple as doing body weight exercises. These would include push-ups, pull-ups, lunges and heel raises. These can also be done with resistance bands.

There are other choices for physical fitness:

- Running
- Hiking
- Bicycling
- Swimming
- Skating/Rollerblading
- Team sports
- Ballroom or other dancing
- And many others

The important thing is to engage in regular physical activities. Do what you enjoy. Do what feels good. Don't overdo it and risk injury. Just do a little more each day, and you'll be on your way.

Physical fitness must be part of your life as you start your business.

Get Your Sleep

Successful people get between 7-8 hours of sleep per night. That is our biology. In the long term, you can't fight your biology.

Scientists are beginning to understand why.

Your brain is only 2% of your body mass, but uses 25% of your total energy. That much brain activity generates high levels of toxins during your waking hours. So how does your brain flush out those toxins?

Researcher Jeff Iliff gave a fascinating TED talk you can watch on TED.com. He explained there is a barrier between the brain and the rest of the body, a protective measure to keep bad stuff out of your brain. But this same barrier keeps toxins trapped in the brain too. Scientists are learning that it's during sleep that the brain flushes out these toxins and cleans itself.

If you don't sleep, the toxins build up, creating that "brain fog" you've probably felt after a red-eye flight or a poor night's sleep. The effects can be the same as that of drugs or alcohol. Many scientists believe this toxic buildup contributes to brain diseases like dementia and Alzheimer's.

My father worked a night shift for decades, and probably never got enough sleep. He was stricken with Alzheimer's, and passed away from complications.

During sleep, the brain also catalogs thoughts and creates the connections of long-term memory. Your dreams are part of that process.

We may have visions of the sleep-deprived entrepreneur, burning the candle at both ends to make their business a success, but productivity is directly tied to sleep. Researcher Dan Ariely found that people are most creative between 2-4 hours after they wake up. With brain fog, it's hard to take advantage of that window.

A bedtime ritual is the best way to prepare for a good night's sleep. Here are some popular rituals:

- Go to bed early.
- Stick to a regular sleep schedule.
- Take melatonin and magnesium two hours before bed.
- Stop looking at blue light screens (TV, computer, smartphone) at least two hours before bed.

- Filter out blue light with special glasses or with special software.

- Make your sleeping area as dark as possible.

- Listen to soothing sounds or music right before bed.

Despite your best efforts, it may be difficult to get the needed 7-8 hours of sleep during the night.

Things happen. In our home, what happens is, like clockwork, our cat wants food and company most mornings around 4am. I get up with him so my wife isn't disturbed, and stay up until he is settled again. Here's a photo of Muggsy.

Because of these early morning interruptions, I'm proud to say I take naps. Naps allow me to get enough sleep and be more productive.

So get your sleep. It's even good for your mental health.

MENTAL HEALTH

Mental health is as important as physical health.

If you have a medical issue such as depression, hopefully you are working with your doctor to address it. If not, I urge you to do so.

There are several things you can do to enhance your mental health.

Spend Time with Others

We are social animals. We need connection and interaction. Just make sure you are spending time with those that bring out the best in you.

Enjoy Hobbies and Interests

Doing what you enjoy is a key to mental health. Especially doing things that put you into Flow. Flow is that sense you get when you are so absorbed in an activity that you lose track of time.

Learning New Things

Positive psychology research has found that a Love of Learning is a key indicator of well-being. We can't stay static. Learning new things expands us and stretches our limits.

Daily Affirmations

Affirmations are like little pep talks you give yourself. These are positive phrases you can read, listen to, or say out loud every day. Remember, it takes three positive doses to counter each negative that bombards you.

Be Grateful

I mentioned this before, but it's worth repeating. An attitude of gratitude is strongly linked to mental health.

Be Present

All we have is this present moment. It's good here in the present. Don't dwell on the past. Don't worry about the future. Stay in the here and now.

Consider Tapping

I don't mean tap dancing, although that's a great physical activity. Tapping is also known as Emotional Freedom Technique (EFT). It combines the mental part of affirmations with the physical part of acupressure to promote mental health. I'll be talking more about tapping in the next chapter on Habits.

Turn Off the TV

Television has made us a passive, captive audience, sitting around, waiting to be entertained. One of the best ways to be active and proactive is to limit your TV time. Don't watch other people's lives; go out and make your own.

No News is Good News

The news today is overwhelmingly sensationalized, polarized, and negative. Headlines seem not to inform, but to trick you into continuing so they can serve you more ads. Avoid news and increase your positive ratio. You'll feel better.

SPIRITUAL HEALTH

The final stop on this health tour is your spiritual health. Too often neglected, there are many ways to promote spiritual health.

Attitude of Gratitude

Gratitude appears again. Being grateful for everything you have is key to your spiritual health as well.

Prayer

Daily prayer is a powerful spiritual force for those with faith.

Spiritual Readings/Daily Affirmations

The source can be the Bible, the Koran, the Torah, the Tao Te Ching, or even a 12-step program. Reading from texts or repeating passages out loud can lift your spirits.

Meditation

Meditation may be the most powerful source of spiritual health. Meditation puts focus on the present, reduces mind chatter, and allows clarity to shine through.

Tim Ferriss, author of the bestselling *Four-Hour Work Week*, says a regular meditation practice is the one common element in over 80% of high performers he has met.

I have been meditating for almost 25 years. Many of my most important insights have come during my daily meditation practice. You are reading this book because I had a personal insight during meditation. Check out the book resource page for meditation resources.

Tai Chi/Chi Kung/Yoga

I group these spiritual practices together because they also share a physical component. Tai Chi has even been called a "moving meditation." I have been practicing Tai Chi and Chi Kung for almost 25 years, and I have recently added a yoga practice.

Enhancing health must be a priority, especially when over 50. The prescription is simple:

- See your doctor
- Watch what you eat
- Stay physically active
- Get your sleep
- Take care of your mind
- Nurture your spirit

The challenge is doing these things on a consistent basis. One thing that can help you get and stay healthy is building positive habits, the topic of our next foundation.

CHAPTER 4 – THE THIRD FOUNDATION: HABITS

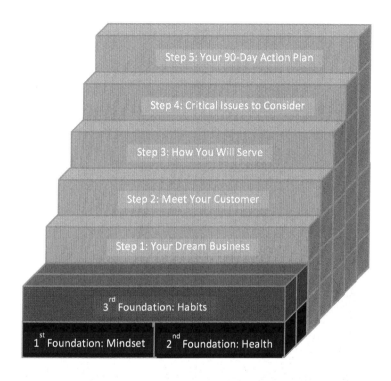

In this chapter, you'll start building your third foundation: your success habits.

You ARE your habits. Good habits move you toward your dreams, while bad habits hold you back.

Like it or not, your life today is a result of the habits you have developed.

Habits are hard to change. It is even more difficult if you are over 50.

But you CAN build new habits.

In this chapter, I'll review the most important science of habits and what the findings mean for you.

Then I'll share THE MOST IMPORTANT thing you must understand about building habits.

Next, I'll show you the easiest, most effective habit you can create for yourself. This habit is universal among successful people. I'll even share what I do.

After that, I'll give you the powerful and proven techniques for getting good habits to stick.

Finally, I'll end the chapter with tips for dealing with bad habits.

The Science Behind Habits

Don't you just hate your bad habits? You know you shouldn't eat that extra dessert. But you do. Then you beat yourself up over it.

Why don't we have the willpower to do what we know we should?

Science tells us that willpower is a limited resource. You only have so much. You can't count on willpower alone to guide you. Your willpower WILL wane, and then, for better or worse, your habits will take over.

Based on the work of Stanford researcher BJ Fogg, habit expert James Clear has come up with what he calls the 3 R's of forming habits:

1. **Reminder.** The reminder is the trigger that initiates the behavior. In the case of the dessert, maybe it's seeing an ad for ice cream. The ad convinces you that you want ice cream.

2. **Routine.** The routine is the behavior itself. In the case of the dessert, maybe it's going to the freezer to get the ice cream and then eating it. Routines can happen with very little thought or with lots of rationalizations.

3. **Reward.** The reward is the benefit you gain from the behavior. The ice cream tastes good, and you enjoyed getting a treat. But sometimes anticipation is the reward, not the actual treat itself.

Habits require these three steps, reminder, routine, and reward, in that order.

HABITS AND THE BRAIN

Does it seem more difficult to change habits as you get older? Brain research tells us this is true. Habits are one "new trick" it IS harder to teach an "old dog."

Loretta Breuning is an expert on mammal behavior. In her book, *Habits of a Happy Brain: Retrain your brain to boost your serotonin, dopamine, oxytocin, and endorphin levels*, Dr. Breuning describes that habits are created by building specific neural pathways in the brain. Most pathways are created by the time we are around 20 years old. Childhood and adolescence is when the brain easily creates new pathways.

These brain pathways are reinforced every time they are used. They become the brain's preferred paths and shortcuts to predictable outcomes.

Building better habits means rewiring the brain to create new pathways. Neuroplasticity shows us this is possible, but overriding the brain's superhighways that were paved decades ago is a challenge.

Habits don't change instantly, but some research suggests you can rewire your brain for new habits in as little as 21 days. The problem is willpower can only do so much for you.

The good news is all you need is a Slight Edge.

THE SLIGHT EDGE

I'm now going to share THE MOST IMPORTANT idea in this entire book:

Success happens when you take advantage of the Slight Edge.

The phrase "The Slight Edge" comes from Jeff Olson's book of the same name.

The Slight Edge is simply the cumulative effect of consistent, small actions over a long period of time.

Time is going to pass. If you consistently work every day on the small things to create a better habit, you will succeed.

If you consistently do nothing or worse every day, at best you'll be stuck right where you are.

The paradox is that what you do on any given day may have little or no effect, but the *cumulative* effects over long periods of time are momentous.

Let me illustrate how The Slight Edge has worked with my nutrition plan over the last six months.

I had been obsessing over my nutrition and my weight for decades. I had tried everything at least once. A few years ago, I even tried a nutrition plan meant for bodybuilders, which was laughable considering my physique at the time. I was able to lose 25 pounds over a two-year period, but it wasn't sustainable and I gained everything back.

In mid-February 2015, I finally took 100% responsibility for my nutrition. The changes I made to my diet were described in the previous chapter. Unlike my previous attempts, this is a new healthy eating lifestyle I know I'll be able to stick to for the rest of my life.

I also weighed myself every day to keep a record and to keep myself accountable. Here is a graph of my daily weight loss over that time:

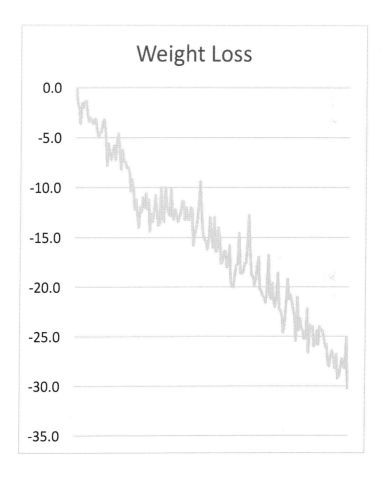

You can see I have lost over 30 pounds in six months. This isn't an overnight success, but it shows the cumulative effective of my Slight Edge dietary shift compounding over time.

Note there are several upward spikes in the graph. Those were my "Free Days" when I took a break from my plan. The largest upward spike was a weekend trip to Reno when I enjoyed three All-You-Can-Eat Buffets in two days! But the Slight Edge difference was that I owned every upward spike, and IMMEDIATELY returned to my plan.

This is the power of building habits with the Slight Edge.

We will re-visit The Slight Edge later in the book when you build your 90-day Action Plan.

So when it comes to habits – dream big, but start small.

DAILY PRACTICE

There is a secret habit I want to share with you. This is a habit I have been following for a long time, and one that's practiced by most successful people.

This habit is an active morning ritual.

It seems simple. (And it is.)

But it is profound.

I have always called my morning ritual my "Daily Practice."

The Daily Practice is the series of things you do to begin your day. Ideally, these are things that nurture you, start your day with a sense of accomplishment, and build momentum for you to do great things all day long.

Best-selling author James Altucher's Daily Practice consists of only four things:

1. Physical – take a walk every day
2. Mental – come up with 10 new ideas every day
3. Emotional – spend time with positive people
4. Spiritual – be grateful for your life

My own Daily Practice includes a few more activities, but I've added to it over time. You can start with as many or as few of these as you like.

Below is My Daily Practice. For each Daily Practice activity below, I have included my rewards from each habit.

My Daily Practice:

- Gratitude reflection – build a positive attitude

- Make the bed – discipline

- Yoga – flexibility, calmness, focus

- 30+ minute meditation – calmness, focus, activate inner wisdom

- Daily readings – inspiration, grounding

- Speak affirmations out loud – reinforce positive intentions

- Tapping/Emotional Freedom Technique (EFT) – uncover fears and counter them

- Review written goals – reinforce my positive direction

- Chi Kung/Tai Chi – moving meditation, calmness, focus

My Daily Practice takes just over an hour. I can't always do it all at once to start my day. Life happens. But you can be sure that by the end of each day, I have done every single one of these activities. Day in and day out.

Create YOUR personal Daily Practice. To start, James Clear recommends you answer the following question: What is the one thing that—when you do it—the rest of your day seems to go better?

GETTING HABITS TO STICK

You are now fired up to start building positive habits that will take you toward your goals and dreams. These are the habits to help you start your dream business.

But how do you get habits to stick?

Let me share the findings from research and best practices.

Habits Come from Identity

Habits that stick must be based on your identity of YOU; how you see yourself.

Only YOU can define your identity. You get to decide who you are. It does NOT have to be how you currently see yourself.

First do your identity work.

Model your identity after others you admire and aspire to be like. What are their defining characteristics?

Take those characteristics to be your own. Start with one characteristic at a time, and reinforce that characteristic with positive self-talk.

Believe in yourself.

Do what a person with that characteristic would do. Start small. Try to do it every time. Do it again and again. Be consistent. Don't quit if you slip up. Just do it right the next time.

Let's take the example of my dental care.

I had a horrible track record. Other than brushing my teeth most days, I had no good habits. A decade might pass between visits to the dentist. This was with good dental insurance! And oddly enough, I wasn't afraid of visiting the dentist; I just never went.

About five years ago, I read about all the scary health problems that can arise from poor dental care. It wasn't pretty.

My teeth felt fine, but I didn't want to be that old guy with no teeth. Not if I could help it.

So I made a change in my identity.

I said to myself: "I am that guy who takes regular care of his teeth." Notice the focus is on who I *am* and what I *do*.

I took the next small step: I found a local dentist.

I took the next small step: I made an appointment.

I took the next small step: I went to the appointment.

That first cleaning was a horrible experience. My eyes were closed, and I think they had to use jackhammers to remove the plaque buildup!

How did I survive? Turns out, it was another habit to the rescue.

Remember my nearly twenty-five-year meditation practice? During the teeth cleaning, I just used that habit to put myself in a calm meditative state. I focused on my breathing. Soon the cleaning was over.

I was lucky. My teeth and gums were fine. At the end, the dentist told me the same thing I'd heard at every other dental appointment: brush, floss, and mouth rinse every day.

But now my identity is "that guy who takes regular care of his teeth."

Then I took the next small step. On the way home, I bought mouth rinse and a package of handled flossers (easier for me than using dental floss). I put these items together on the bathroom counter right next to the toothbrush and toothpaste. I created my "dental care station" where I couldn't miss it.

I brushed, flossed, and rinsed that night. I repeated the habit the next day. And the day after that. Soon I was "that guy who takes regular care of his teeth." I later upped my game with an electric toothbrush. It has a prominent place in my dental care station. I also visit the dentist at least twice per year.

If I can keep this habit for five years, I can do ANYTHING!

You can do anything too! Decide what is important to you. Decide *who* you want to be. Then prove it to yourself with small wins. Set yourself up for consistent, repeatable, positive actions over time.

That is the power of habits.

Don't Break the Chain

Habits stick when you don't break the chain. Do it every time.

Writing a book is hard! Trust me. I had to put in the work.

When I started my blog, TheMaturEntrepreneur.com, I made a personal commitment to post every day, no matter what. This built my new habit of consistent writing. With over 250 blog posts so far, I haven't broken the chain yet.

I built that blog writing habit into a book writing habit. I made a personal commitment to write at least 2 hours per day until my first draft was finished. I even marked an X on the calendar each day to reinforce the habit. I never broke the chain. This book is the result.

Know the Destination, but Focus on the Journey

Habits stick when you focus on the right things. Your identity sets the direction. You must then focus on the here and now. What will you do RIGHT NOW to move toward that identity? What is the next small step? Focus only on that next small step and do it. Then repeat.

As it says in the Tao Te Ching: *A journey of 1,000 miles starts with a single step.*

Become Accountable

Share your goals and habits with others for accountability. Let others help you create the habits you want. Accountability partners, mastermind groups, or coaches can also do this more formally.

Dealing with Slip-ups

To err is human. Welcome to the human race.

As you build new habits, there will be slip-ups. Expect them. Plan for them.

Do things that reinforce habits. Write down your new identity. Read it regularly. Reading it out loud is even more powerful. Make it part of your Daily Practice affirmations. Visualize your success.

A single slip-up won't matter, IF you do the next right thing.

Bad habits

How do you lose bad habits?

Start with identity. I'm sorry, but that bad habit you're thinking about reflects your current identity. But does that bad habit reflect who you *want* to be? Think of losing a bad habit as getting back to being you.

Remember those superhighways in your brain? You don't eliminate a bad habit, but rather you need to replace it by building a new pathway in your brain. It takes time and effort, but mostly perseverance.

James Clear recommends using "but" to overcome negative self-talk. Five years ago, I said to myself: "I'm not taking good care of my teeth right now, **but** I can become that guy."

Eliminate triggers. If you can't resist candy, don't have candy in plain view.

Find substitutes. Like keeping fresh fruit in the kitchen instead of candy.

A FINAL WORD ON HABITS

You are your habits.

I hope you now understand that your life today is the result of your past habits, and that habits reflect your self-identity.

It's time for new positive habits that reflect the identity YOU want. The identity YOU get to choose.

Now you've learned the 3 Foundations for Success:

- Your Success Mindset
- Your Health
- Your Habits

It's time to start YOUR dream business.

Let's take the first step.

CHAPTER 5 – STEP 1: YOUR DREAM BUSINESS

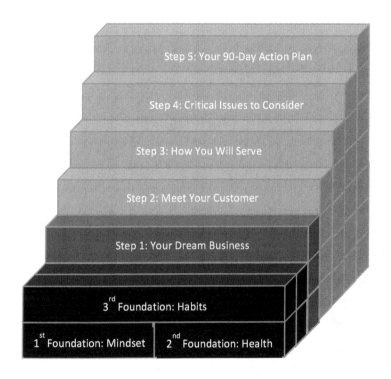

In this chapter, you'll learn how to discover your dream business.

I'll share a step-by-step process to uncover the business you were meant to run based on what is important to YOU.

Since the Connected Economy makes almost any business type possible, we'll start with an introduction to the variety of businesses to consider.

Then you'll search for YOUR dream business by developing options that match your purpose and passion.

When you've captured all your potential options, the next section shows you how to narrow down to your best options. You'll be able to prioritize them based on criteria that are unique to you and evaluate your business options using a simple scorecard.

By the end of this section, if you complete the work, you'll have discovered YOUR best option.

THE DIFFERENT TYPES OF BUSINESSES

Let's spur your thinking by considering a few of the different types of businesses.

Freelancer

A freelancer typically has one set of skills or expertise that they offer to numerous clients. They build a reputation for that one skill and become a go-to resource when someone needs help in that area. An example would be a freelance graphic designer. When people want things like a logo or a book cover, they often choose a freelance graphic designer to do that specific work.

The number of freelancers and the variety of services offered is growing rapidly with the Connected Economy. Websites like upwork.com and fiverr.com are worldwide marketplaces where freelancers and clients can connect for projects.

Virtual Business

A virtual business exists only on the Internet. Products and services are only offered online; there are no brick and mortar stores. There are literally millions of virtual businesses that address various niche markets. The oldest virtual businesses are only 20 years old.

New Local Business

In this case, you see a need in your local market. You then create a business from scratch to meet that need. An example might be starting a new local restaurant with a specific cuisine.

Existing Business

This is the case where you purchase and take over the ownership of an existing business.

Franchise

A common path for first-time business owners is to purchase and run a franchise. An example would be owning a local Subway sandwich shop.

Investment Property Owner

Investing in commercial or residential real estate is a popular way to diversify your nest egg and build long-term wealth. You buy and manage properties that you rent out.

Social Entrepreneurship

Is there some social issue that you feel must be addressed?

Gandhi said, "Be the change you want to see in the world."

In the Connected Economy, your desire for social change can become a business. Doing this can be extremely gratifying, and building wealth may become secondary.

DEFINING YOUR DREAM BUSINESS

You've seen the variety of business options you can consider. Now is the time to start zeroing in on what may be right for you.

Do you already have an idea about your business? That's great. But it's also valuable to go through this process to make sure you've considered all your options.

What Is Your WHY?

The most important questions you need to ask are:

- Why do you want to start a business?
- What is your vision for your business?
- What is your vision for your life?

Think about what YOU want and WHY you want it.

My WHY is to inspire and support people over 50 to start their own business, while creating a business that offers the lifestyle I desire.

YOUR PASSIONS

Once you know your WHY, consider your passions. A business aligning with your passions gives you that something extra to keep your enthusiasm high during the journey.

Consider this quote from Howard Thurman:

"Don't ask what the world needs. Ask what makes you come alive, and go do it. Because what the world needs is people who have come alive."

There are a few ways to uncover your passions.

Flow

Think about experiences when time seemed to stand still for you. When you're "in the zone," actions seem easy, effortless, and enjoyable. This is being in a state of Flow.

You are at your most productive when in Flow. The rest of the world seems to fall away. You enjoy tremendous focus.

Consider keeping a Flow journal. Document those times when you felt in the zone. What were you doing? What was the subject? Over time, you may begin to see patterns emerge of things that are common to your Flow experiences.

Back to Your Childhood

Think about what got you excited as a child and teenager. What were your hobbies and interests then? How did you spend your free time? What activities did you enjoy so much that your parents had to drag you away from them?

Collect these memories in a journal. Again, observe the patterns you see.

Free Time

How do you currently spend your free time? What do you enjoy? Do you have hobbies or other interests? What are your creative pursuits? In the Connected

Economy, hobbies can often turn into business opportunities.

If you keep a journal, you can collect these activities in one place. Add to the list as things come to mind.

Review Your Career Interests

Think about your past and current work. When were you most motivated? What bored you quickly? What things did you hate to do?

Are you a born salesperson? Do you like spreadsheets and details? Do you thrive on building and leading teams? Are you a product person? Or are you at your best performing services?

You should consider playing to your strengths.

Consider the work you currently perform in your present position. Could you perform similar work for a variety of clients? That's how I got started with my first business venture. My first project as an independent consultant/stay-at-home dad was completing ongoing tasks as an independent contractor for the consulting firm I had just left.

Do you have interests in industries outside your current position? Could you bring a new perspective as an outsider?

Write down everything that comes to you about your experiences.

Look Outside Yourself

What do you think is wrong with the world? What do you care about? What frustrates you? What do you wish were different? How might you fix things?

Keep a log of your frustrations and your solutions. Add to the list as additional things come to mind.

Who Are Your Mentors?

Another source of inspiration is mentors. Do you know and admire certain individuals who are where you want to be someday? Find out everything you can about them. Find out how they got to where they are. Find out what you can do to get there too.

Do What You Love

I know it sounds cliché. But now is the time to consider simply doing what you love.

John Gardner coined the phrase "repotting" many years ago. This is the idea of making a career change every few years. You've learned a lot over the years. In the Connected Economy, you can build a business from that. Your options may include:

- Teaching
- Coaching
- Speaking
- Consulting
- Writing
- And many others

Next to each option, make a note of which category it falls under. The categories are the points of inspiration we discussed a moment ago, such as:

- Flow
- Childhood Interests
- Free Time Interests

- Career Interests

- Looking Outside Yourself

- Based On Mentors

- What You Love to Do

EXPAND YOUR OPTIONS

Don't make a decision right now. Just collect options. Take a few hours to get them out of your head and write them down. Next, look over these options at least a couple times to set your intention.

Keep your lists handy for the next few days. Add to them when something new comes to mind.

Look for Patterns

You'll have a solid set of options after your subconscious does its work.

Now is the time to look for patterns within the options.

Do some options appear in multiple categories? These options should move to the top of your list.

For example, say you like to write. Writing might have been a childhood interest. When writing, you may lose track of time while in flow. Writing would be an option that fits multiple categories.

Do you see any patterns in the options? Can several options be combined?

As an example, say marketing is an option based on your career interests. Let's also say that coaching is another option for you based on your interests. You could combine those options into a business as a marketing coach.

Understand Your Commitment

The rewards of starting your business are great, but starting a business is not without risks. Understanding your commitment is critical.

What is your risk tolerance? Are you ready to jump in right now with both feet? Do you want to follow your passion completely?

Or do you feel more comfortable starting small? I have chosen such a path for myself.

How much time, money, and other resources are you prepared to commit? Consider the following graph:

	Low Financial	High Financial
High Time	**Sweat Equity**	**All-In**
Low Time	**Need a LONG time**	**Hands Off**

Where would you place yourself on this graph?

Let's consider the four major quadrants:

1. Small time commitment, Small financial commitment –Building a viable business will require a LONG time.

2. Large time commitment, Small financial commitment – Business choices must reflect the value of "sweat equity." Expect that the business must grow organically, and will be

constrained by your efforts and your ability to reinvest profits.

3. Small time commitment, Large financial commitment – You must be comfortable with a hands-off approach, playing a role more like an investor and advisor. Accept that others will be running your business.

4. Large time commitment, Large financial commitment – This is the "all-in" scenario. You will be giving your all to your dreams. This quadrant has higher reward potential, but also higher risk, depending how you manage the process.

Make sure you select the quadrant that best matches your personal situation.

You must truly understand the time commitment you are willing to make. You already have many things that require your time and attention, such as family, friends, community, work, etc. Be realistic.

Entrepreneur Nick Loper uses the term "side hustle" for a business that you start on the side. Side hustles are a popular way for busy people to begin. Of course, for many people the goal of a side hustle is to eventually grow enough to become the primary source of income.

Multiple Income Streams

Laser-like focus is critical in the beginning. You must avoid the "bright, shiny objects" that will try to draw your attention.

However, a longer-term goal should be multiple income streams. Keeping all your eggs in one basket is dangerous. For example, a consultant might also be a coach, a speaker, and an author. I've heard that the average multi-millionaire has at least seven separate sources of income.

The best income streams are known as passive income. Passive income results from your hard work in the past, but not directly from your current efforts. Think of passive income as making money while you sleep or while you are on vacation.

This book is a source of passive income for me. I worked extremely hard to research and write it, but now that it's released, I earn author royalties every time someone buys it. Even while I sleep! (So thank you for that!)

Narrow Down Options

Now that you've brainstormed a large list of potential business ideas, it's time to narrow down your options.

Think about what criteria are important to you. I recommend that the most important criterion be your WHY, but it is up to you. Come up with as many criteria as you feel are important. Prioritize these criteria based on their relative importance to you. Place the most important criterion at the top of the list.

Consider creating a scorecard with your prioritized criteria in the first column. Then have separate columns for each option.

For each option, determine how well that option fits within each of the criteria.

Use the following:

BLACK – great fit

DARK GRAY – good fit

LIGHT GRAY – poor fit

Next, select all the options that match your #1 criterion. Discard the others.

The options in the scorecard were selected because of their fit with your #1 criterion. Make them all BLACKs. Now fill out the scorecard for each option relative to the other criteria.

Below is an example of a completed scorecard with six criteria and four options:

	Option A	Option B	Option C	Option D
Criterion #1				
Criterion #2				
Criterion #3				
Criterion #4				
Criterion #5				
Criterion #6				

Looking at each of the options in this example scorecard, it appears that Option D is the best choice. Option D has the most BLACKs at the top, and no LIGHT GRAYs. Option A appears to be the second best choice.

REALISTIC EXPECTATIONS

Starting your business will be more rewarding than you can imagine, but you still need realistic expectations.

Your life will change dramatically, and you must be prepared.

Envision your ideal business:

- What are your revenues?
- Do you have employees?
- How much are you earning?
- How much investment is required upfront?
- What is your lifestyle like?
- Where are you living and working?
- What will you do day-to-day?

- How much depends on you personally?
- Other factors?

What are you willing to give up in your current life to start and run your business? What changes and sacrifices will you have to make?

MY STORY

Unfortunately, I didn't start with my WHY. It took me a while to get there.

I started with my skills:

- Analysis
- Engineering
- Building organizations
- Dealing with complexity

Next were my interests:

- Climate change
- Sustainable agriculture
- Internet of Things (IoT)
- Big Data applications

I started heading down the typical MBA entrepreneurship path. I was trained to find a "billion-dollar idea," create a business plan that would attract funding, and build a company. In this model of entrepreneurship, you'd work extremely hard for several years, and then hope for a successful exit.

But that path wasn't my WHY.

My WHY came to me in two insights.

The first insight into my WHY was that it wasn't about me. It had to be about my customers. I had to care about those I wanted to serve.

I am passionate about local, sustainable agriculture. Eating well enhances our health and quality of life, so my thought was to build a business to help local farmers.

Then during a meditation, I had an "aha moment." As I was focusing on my breathing, a thought appeared:

"You need to help mature entrepreneurs."

This was the second insight into my WHY.

So I started my blog,
www.TheMaturEntrepreneur.com. I wanted to
document my journey serving local farmers. I also
wanted to inspire my generation to become
entrepreneurs. I wrote and posted something every day.

After several months, I reviewed my posts. Some were
about local growers, but most were about inspiring and
supporting those over 50 who wanted to start their own
business.

My WHY is inspiring and supporting those over 50
who want to start their business!

I thought about criteria outside my WHY. The major
criteria for me were lifestyle and opportunities to learn
and grow.

My option #1 was serving local growers. My option #2
was serving Mature Entrepreneurs.

Below is the scorecard for my options and my criteria:

	Serving Local Growers	Serving Mature Entrepreneurs
My WHY		
Lifestyle		
Learn and Grow		

Serving YOU became the obvious choice for me. It fit my WHY perfectly. It's a green light for the other criteria.

Inspiring and supporting YOU became a no-brainer for me. I wanted to share everything I've learned about starting a business when over 50. I wanted YOU to know about the new opportunities in the Connected Economy.

I want to inspire and support YOU!

I want YOU to start your dream business. Just like me.

This book is my start.

In this chapter, we introduced a process to uncover your dream business based on what is important to YOU. Now that you've narrowed down your selections and heard the story of how I arrived at my dream business, the next thing you need is a customer.

CHAPTER 6 – STEP 2: MEET YOUR CUSTOMER

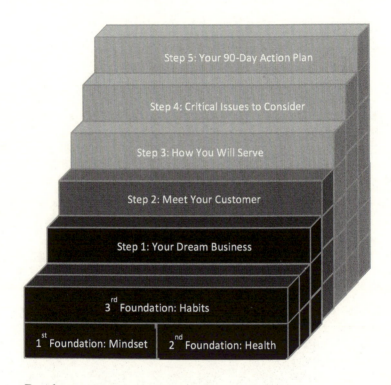

Ready to meet your customer?

In the previous chapter, you learned a process to find your dream business. The cool part is it was always there waiting for you; you just needed to dig a bit to uncover it.

But businesses are not charities. Businesses must make profits to survive and thrive, and profits come from customers.

Let's find yours.

In this chapter, you'll learn how to define and understand your ideal customer, and how to use that understanding.

DEFINING YOUR IDEAL CUSTOMER

Defining your ideal customers is hard. Not everyone does it, but it's worth doing to save yourself heartache and confusion down the road.

Many first-time entrepreneurs want to serve everyone. You love your business, and you want everyone else to love it like you do.

But here is the truth: if you try to appeal to everyone, you end up attracting NO ONE!

It's like companies who say their target market is everyone in the US. They hope to get a small 1% share of that market. That's 3 million customers!

It sounds great on the surface, but it is exceedingly difficult for a new business to have both a broad enough appeal to reach that many customers and the marketing budget necessary to do so.

Think about being a customer yourself.

You have a limited amount of attention. Research shows you are bombarded with thousands of marketing messages each day. That's a lot of noise. What's the best way to cut through all that noise?

A message that seems to be created just for YOU. A message that resonates personally.

Customers are not cattle. Show them some respect. Treat them like individuals.

One size does not fit all.

But how do you treat every potential customer like an individual?

You can't. Don't bother trying.

What you can do is define your ideal customer, and then build your business for that ideal customer.

This is the most important thing you can do.

You need to identify a niche.

One way is to find the intersection of multiple groups. For example, my niche is YOU. As shown in the following diagram:

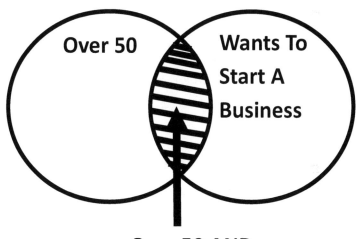

**Over 50 AND
Wants To Start A Business**

Your Customer Avatar

Creating your Customer Avatar is the most important strategy for a successful business.

For the rest of the chapter I'll use the term "Avatar" as shorthand for "Customer Avatar."

So, who is your Avatar?

Your Avatar is simply a characterization of the ideal customer you want to serve. Your Avatar isn't a real person, but it can help if you imagine your Avatar as if they are a living breathing customer.

Let's walk through an example of a customer Avatar. In this case, we'll even give her a name: Ava. If Ava encountered your business, she would immediately become the best customer you could ever have because your business is built precisely for her. The products are for Ava. The services are for Ava. The marketing messages are directed at Ava. It's all geared toward Ava.

Are YOU your own Avatar? If your dream business matches your WHY and will be built on your passions and interests, you likely have many characteristics of your Avatar. So your own ideas are a good place to start.

There are three levels that must be considered to define your Avatar:

1. Demographic
2. Psychographic
3. Emotional

Level One: Demographic

The first level of information you want to compile is demographic. These are the top-level facts about your Avatar.

Following is a list of typical demographic data that can be compiled:

- Age
- Gender
- Marital status
- Where they live
- Work experience
- Education level
- Income level
- Type of job
- Languages spoken
- Appearance
- Health
- Finances
- Family
- Employer
- Job Type

Level Two: Psychographic

The psychographic profile of your Avatar would include elements of their personality, values, opinions, attitudes, interests, and lifestyle.

Following is a list of typical psychographic information that can be compiled:

- Hobbies/interests
- Offline and online hangouts
- Information sources
- Influencers
- Group memberships
- Clothing choices
- Fitness level
- Workday activities
- Their values – conservative or liberal, religious or not, etc.
- Volunteer positions
- Give to charity
- World view
- Optimistic or pessimistic
- Growth or fixed mindset
- Favorite brands
- News sources
- TV habits
- Movies

- Types of vacation
- Favorite books, magazines, music
- Authors, teachers or experts followed
- Mentors

Level Three: Emotional

It is valuable to go beyond demographics and psychographics. Consider your Avatar's deepest thoughts and fears at an emotional level.

Following is a list of typical questions to ask about your Avatar as you complete this exercise:

- What is their WHY?
- What do they already know about you?
- What do they already know about your business?
- Are they a customer of your competitors?
- What are their needs, wants, and motivations?
- What keeps your avatar up at night?
- What are their hopes, dreams, fears, and frustrations?
- What does it feel like to be them?
- What are their personal goals?
- What are their family goals?
- What else has your avatar already tried to do in order to solve their problem?

- What are they talking about with their family?
- What objections could they have?
- How do they make their decisions?
- What else are they buying?
- What are their pain points?

Consider questions they may have about their work:

- What are their business goals?
- Do they love their work?
- Does their work still satisfy them?
- Has their work become purely to get paid and to support their family?
- Are they struggling with their workload, or just coasting?
- Are they disappointed by a lack of challenge in their work?
- Are they worried about losing their job?
- Are they working at more than one job just to pay the bills?

Be as specific as you can about their WHY, because it will often play a big role in the choices they make, and in their foundational mindset, health, and work habits. Doing this exercise helps you get inside the head of your ideal customer and truly understand their pain points and potential decision and motivational factors.

Benefits of Knowing Your Avatar

When your business is new, gaining trust will be job #1 for you. This has to come BEFORE you have actual paying customers, because customers have to TRUST you before they'll pay you for anything.

You gain trust by providing compelling value and helpful information. By letting your Avatar drive your value and information strategy, customers will instantly feel like they belong. Offer consistent messages that resonate with customers that match your Avatar profile.

Because you are speaking directly to them, you become the obvious choice for them. You make them feel understood. You reinforce who they are and who they want to be.

Your Avatar can also drive decisions on the products and services you provide.

Selling will become easier. After all, you will just be giving customers what they want.

Your marketing will result in:

- Better leads
- Higher conversion of leads
- Faster conversion of leads
- Fewer customer complaints

USING YOUR AVATAR

Create your Avatar to the level of detail that makes sense to you. Compile information about your ideal customer that applies to the business you want to create.

Read your Avatar profile often to keep your finger on the pulse of your customers.

Consider creating a short story about your Avatar. Review the story on a regular basis.

After creating your Avatar, ask yourself the following questions:

- Is there a business opportunity? Do they have pain points? Can you solve them?
- If you offer a product or service, can they pay?
- Do you think they will pay?

If the answer to any of these questions is NO, you may need to rethink your direction.

Use your Avatar to ask and answer questions you may have about your customers' issues:

- What problems they have that make them an ideal for your business?
- What are they secretly afraid of?
- What is the worst thing that could happen if they DON'T solve their problem?
- What would that mean to them?
- What would that mean to their family?
- What would that mean to their friends?
- How might their lifestyle change?
- What would be the financial implications?
- What would be the career implications?
- What is the BEST outcome if their problem IS solved?
- How would they view the perfect solution?
- What do they really want?
- What would they be willing to pay for a solution?
- How can your business meet their real needs and desires?

If your business is aimed at people like you, it's easy to put yourself in your Avatar's shoes:

- What do you fear about your own life?
- What keeps you up at night?
- What stresses you out?
- What do you find yourself avoiding because of fear?
- How do you think others would react if they found out about your fears?
- What might happen if your fears get worse?
- What do you secretly wish could change about your situation?
- What is the dream solution that you'd pay almost anything for?
- What is the story of that dream solution unfolding?
- How will others respond if you fix this situation?
- With the situation fixed, what opportunities open up for you?

Your Avatar can direct you where to learn more about potential customers. Go to the places where you can find and interact with customers. Such as:

- Their social media sites
- Websites they frequent
- Groups for which they are members

- Organizations for which they belong
- Places where they have fun

Interacting with potential customers on their turf will allow you to better understand them, update your Avatar, and serve them best.

If your plans involve business-to-business (B2B), create an Avatar for the decision-makers in your target companies.

We covered some very important concepts in this chapter.

Defining your ideal customer is the most important thing you can do to differentiate your business.

I hope you see the critical importance of your Avatar. Next up, I'll show you how you can find out ways to best serve your customers.

CHAPTER 7 – STEP 3: HOW YOU WILL SERVE

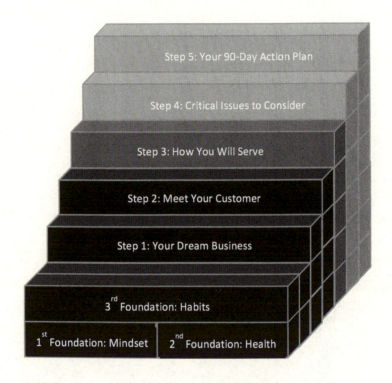

In Step 1, you found your dream business.

Next, you defined your ideal customer.

Now the question to ask is:

How can my business serve that ideal customer?

This chapter starts by making the case for an attitude of service. I'll show you specific things that successful businesses do to serve.

The chapter ends with preparing a Vision Statement and Mission Statement to communicate and focus future efforts.

THE CASE FOR SERVICE

Back in the First Foundation, I talked about a Mindset of Service. A Mindset of Service naturally leads to a business of service.

Remember my "aha moment" during meditation, when I discovered I wanted to serve over-50 entrepreneurs?

Everything changed for me after that.

I'm advocating a customer-focused business. Make your business about your customers. I'm not alone in thinking that way.

Marketing guru Jay Abraham goes so far as to say you shouldn't even use the word "Customer," but that you should use "Client" instead. "Client" implies that you have their best interests at heart. You see yourself as their trusted advisor.

This means taking a long view of the relationship. No longer is it just about making money today. No longer is it about the next transaction or the next sale; it's about providing what's best for them.

What they want. What they need.

Wired magazine founder Kevin Kelly writes about the idea of 1,000 true fans. In the Connected Economy, that's all you need for a sustainable business. Find 1,000 or more true fans. Keep them happy by offering them your best service year after year.

Successful people know this and do this. It's what's best for their businesses too.

HOW TO SERVE

Here are some of the things successful people do to better serve their customers.

Start by Joining Your Customers

Everyone starts their business from scratch with zero customers. You are no different.

You want your ideal customers to find you so they can become your actual customers, but you have to find *them* first.

You need to join them where they already are and begin interacting with them.

Think about where to find your customers. Ask questions such as:

- What are their other interests? How do they learn more about those interests?
- What websites do they visit often?
- What social media sources do they frequent?
- What online forums do they visit?
- Which other experts or influencers do they follow?
- What events do they attend?

This is easier if you are your own Avatar. If so, ask yourself the same questions.

Compile the answers into a file for future reference.

Frequent those same sites and attend those events yourself. Start by just observing. The goal at first is to learn more about your ideal customers.

Understand the ideas that seem to be important there. Get comfortable with the language they use, the trends in the industry, and any insights you discover. Did anything surprise you from embedding yourself in your customer's natural habitat?

Collect all this information and insights for future use.

After you become comfortable in your customer's world, it's time to become active.

Become of service in your customer's world. Attend events. Comment on threads. Offer encouragement to others. Provide value through your interactions. Become a trusted person.

Gain trust first. Then offer value. Remember, at this point we're not trying to sell anything yet.

See the response. Do your ideas resonate with your customers? Is there interest and engagement, or are your ideas greeted with silence or hostility? Make adjustments as necessary so that your messages do resonate. Or maybe a change to your Avatar is needed.

The goal is to become trusted in your customer's world. After you become a known quantity there, you can invite them to your world.

CREATE YOUR WORLD

There are a number of things you can create in your world to serve potential customers.

First up, you'll need a website. Even if your dream business is rooted in the physical world, your website will be a way customers find you, learn about you, and learn to trust you.

And in the Connected Economy, your website can BE your business. This wasn't possible just a few years ago.

So what should your website have? Look around at other sites for best practices, specifically other sites where you find customers. Use them as potential models for your site.

Consider websites that you like or websites that are already doing what you'd like to do.

Your most important consideration should be the user experience. If people don't have a great experience on your site, they may not come back.

You will want to build a community through your website. One of the most important ways is to convince people to join your email list. This is how you can begin a conversation with them. By giving you their email address, they have given you permission to contact them.

Creating an email list can be the subject of an entire book. You must offer something of value to your visitor in exchange for them giving you their email address. Offer them something valuable and FREE. This is often called an "ethical bribe." You must also explicitly assure them that their email address is safe with you, and that they won't be receiving spam because of joining your list. See the book resource page for more.

BUILD TRUST

Building trust will be the first "service" you offer
visitors to your site. Trust is the most important benefit
you can offer potential customers.

But how do you build trust?

Unfortunately, trust does not come easily or quickly.

The best way to build trust is to offer people value for
FREE. If your product is food, you can build trust by
offering free samples. If your service is information,
you can build trust by giving people valuable
information for FREE.

Remember the Golden Rule. How do you like to be
treated? If someone consistently offers you quality
information for free, you will be much more likely to
buy something from them later.

Internet entrepreneur Gary Vaynerchuk coined the
following phrase:

Give, Give, Give, Give, Give... ASK!

Gary builds trust over time with several quality Gives.
In one of his early businesses, he produced a weekly

free video series about wine. He built amazing trust and credibility with his audience, such that when he Asked them to buy wine, they did so without hesitation.

Give your best stuff. Show potential customers how valuable your stuff is.

LISTEN TO YOUR CUSTOMERS

When starting your business, it's natural to feel like you are the expert. But really your customers are the experts. They are the experts in what THEY want and need!

Success is pretty simple: it's finding out what your customers want and need, and then offering it to them.

The best method is simply to listen to them. Let them tell you what they want.

Listen with a beginner's mind. Don't filter what you hear through your experiences.

You listened and learned back when you were visiting their world. Keep listening once they are in your world.

Ask Your Customers

After you've listened, then you can have a conversation. Talk *with* your customers. Don't talk at them.

One way is to create content that might later become a product or service. Ask them how they feel about it.

Another way to collect market intelligence is to survey your email list and those who visit your site.

Ask them what they need and want. Let them tell you their problems. Let them share their pain points. Empathize with them.

Then create products and services they want and need.

The alternative is to just guess at what customers want and need. This path has you spending lots of time and money upfront and then hoping your customers will buy.

Which tactic is more likely to succeed?

RETHINK HOW YOU OFFER

You have to put your products in customers' hands. Let customers use your products and try out your services. Only then you can learn and make the next version even better.

You need what's called a Minimum Viable Product (MVP). Think of an MVP as a quick and dirty version of your eventual product. It's fast and easy to create and easy to use.

Let customers use your MVP. Play with it. Kick the tires. Give you feedback.

That feedback is gold! They tell you what they like about it and more importantly what they DON'T like about it. They tell you what your MVP needs but doesn't have. That way, you don't waste time creating features your customers don't value.

And these early adopters can become your biggest fans. They helped shape the final product. They have skin in the game.

Customers with skin in the game often become evangelists for your business. They like your product.

120

They tell five friends. Those five friends each tell five of their friends.

The best marketing is happy customers who share.

Build a Community

Try to take it up a notch and build a community. Seth Godin calls this building a Tribe.

A community has a different dynamic. You become the leader of the community. But interactions no longer have to involve you directly because community members can interact with each other.

To start a community, you must be clear about what you stand for. Be specific. Be unique. This will attract community members you want.

Then you need to create a home for your community. One option is a forum within your website. Facebook and LinkedIn groups are also growing in popularity, since most members are already active users of such social media sites.

There are numerous tactics for creating a community. Following are some things to consider:

- Ease of joining
- Ease of sharing with others
- Ease of navigating around the community
- Clear rules for behavior
- Content that keeps people engaged
- Ability to grow and scale as the number of members grows

Most important is to listen to the community. You may be the leader, but the community is about them. Give the community what it wants. Allow the direction to change.

VISION AND MISSION

You need to focus your efforts. You need to be explicit about serving your customers. Most effective is creating a Vision Statement and a Mission Statement.

Vision Statement

You put a flag in the ground with your Vision Statement. It's about who you aspire to be in the future, what you want to have achieved, and where you want to go. The Vision is your future destination.

Consider the following structure for your Vision Statement:

My Vision is + <what you aspire to be> + <what you aspire to do> + <who you will serve> + <what is their issue>.

As an example, here is my Vision Statement:

My Vision is to be a recognized leader inspiring and supporting people over 50 who want to start their own business.

Mission Statement

The Mission Statement says the steps you are going to take to realize your Vision. The Mission is the path to your destination.

Consider the following structure for your Mission Statement:

My Mission is + <what you will do or provide> + <who you will serve> + <what is their issue>.

Here is my Mission Statement:

My Mission is to provide resources and services to inspire people over 50 to start their own business, and to support them on their journey.

This book is an example of fulfilling my Mission in support of my Vision.

Using Your Vision and Mission Statements

Constantly refer to your Vision and Mission statement. Make sure every action fits within your Mission. Make sure every action leads you toward your Vision.

I hope you share an attitude of service in your business. Too many businesses focus just on the transaction. Just on the next sale.

When you focus on serving your customers, your business will stand out and be remarkable. And you will realize more success.

Make sure you have a solid Vision and Mission statement. Let them be your guide to choosing the next best thing to do.

In the next step, you decide how to get it all done for your customers.

CHAPTER 8 – STEP 4: CRITICAL ISSUES TO CONSIDER

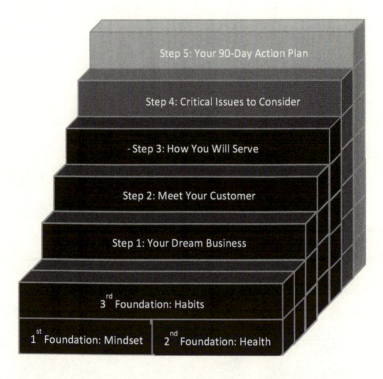

In Step 3, you learned the importance of serving your customers. You also saw some of the things successful businesses do to serve their customers.

In Step 4, we cover critical issues you must consider to serve your customers.

I'll share a framework for getting work done in your business. As the founder, you can't do everything yourself.

We'll cover how to prioritize the challenging work-related issues that inevitably come up in any business, with special emphasis placed on customer-facing issues.

The chapter will close with additional decisions to consider as you start your business.

FRAMEWORK FOR EVALUATING CRITICAL ISSUES

Think about every issue serving customers by asking two questions.

The first question is *How important is this issue in serving your customers?*

If the issue is not important, it deserves less focus. You can't do everything.

For example, many new businesses spend a lot of effort on creating a memorable logo. But in the early stages, is a logo really important to serving your customers?

It's better to work with your customers rather than work on a logo at this time.

If the issue IS important, the second question is *Should I personally take care of this issue, or hire someone to take care of it for me?*

You may not be able to take care of some issues. If a customer needs a website and you don't have those skills, you'll have to get help.

Even if you have the skills, you may want to consider getting help. Again, you can't do everything.

In the Connected Economy, nearly every issue can be outsourced. I've talked about sites such as Upwork.com or Fiverr.com where you can hire freelancers for specific projects. Numerous companies exist to help you with any business function, from finance and accounting, to fulfillment and customer service.

However, any issue that faces the customer MUST be your responsibility. You must either address these issues yourself or closely supervise those who do.

You must personally learn from your customers. Take the long view. Critical information will be lost if you delegate customer contact.

As you start your business, your most important activity is serving customers. In the beginning, it has to be YOU providing valuable content, building your list of potential customers, and gaining their trust. You must be on top of these efforts. Specific tactics may be outsourced, but you must have your finger on the pulse of these activities. Customers must feel like YOU are serving them.

DECIDING WHAT TO SELL

You must also lead the development of your initial products and services. You know your customers better than anyone. You have the relationships, and you know best what they want and need. This personal knowledge will drive the products and services you create. Again, you can always get help from other professionals for specific tasks, but you must lead.

All potential customers have wants and needs. Wants are emotional, while needs are rational. At its simplest, selling is satisfying customer wants and meeting customer needs.

Customers buy to feel good. Customers buy to solve a problem.

Customers care about themselves. Make sure your business reflects this. Make it about THEM.

Your first product or service may need to be small to meet your customers' needs. Customers may need to trust you before spending on higher-cost services.

Make products and services you can sell based on what potential customers tell you. Don't try to make perfect products or services. It can't be done. Reid Hoffman, Founder of LinkedIn, says, "If you are not embarrassed by the first release of your product, you've launched too late."

When you create products and services people want and value, potential customers become actual paying customers. That's when everything changes.

PRICING

A quick word on pricing. Pricing is notoriously difficult. New businesses often undersell themselves by setting a price that is too low. A best practice is to base your price on the value your customer perceives by using your product or service. Remember that value has an emotional component.

My consulting fees were typically based on a high hourly rate for my effort. However, my largest project took into account the value to the client for the results.

What result are customers likely to see by choosing you? What is that result worth to them? Base your pricing on customer benefits, rather than merely your time and materials.

MAKE THAT FIRST SALE

Make that first sale. The first sale is the hardest. You have a real business when a customer votes with their wallet.

The more you do something, whether that's creating content, developing products or services, or making sales, the better you get at it. And the rewarding part for new entrepreneurs is that the biggest learning curve improvements happen in the beginning.

Lead the customer-focused efforts. Serve potential customers. Use their feedback and frustrations to develop and sell initial products.

Gain experience. Learn. Serve the next customer better. Gain more experience. Learn more. Serve the next customer even better. Soon you will have a great business.

As sales increase, then create systems and delegate more responsibility.

HAPPY CUSTOMERS

Happy customers should be your goal.

Happy customers will rave about you to everyone they meet. You can't pay to get that kind of positive exposure. It must be earned.

Happy customers are often willing to provide testimonials that you can use to attract new customers.

Happy customers will tell you how to make your products better and buy more from you later.

THE MOST POWERFUL QUESTIONS TO ASK CUSTOMERS

Constantly ask your customers these most powerful questions:

What's the number one problem you struggle with?

What would you like me to provide for you?

What sorts of things could I provide that you would pay for?

and

I'm thinking of providing XYZ product or service. Will you pre-order it right now?

LIFETIME CUSTOMER VALUE

Lifetime Customer Value is the total profit you will earn from serving someone during their entire time as your customer.

Naturally, happy customers have high Lifetime Customer Value. They provide higher profits with their many purchases, and they also help you reduce the cost to acquire new customers through word of mouth and testimonials.

Happy customers are gold. Treat them well. Nurture them.

Too many businesses fail by ignoring their best customers in search of new customers.

OTHER BUSINESS ISSUES TO CONSIDER

Following are some additional issues that must be considered when starting your business. The importance of each issue depends on your particular situation, as do the methods and tactics to address these issues.

Remember that in the Connected Economy you have more options than you may think. Many companies exist to address such issues for you.

Check the Resources page on my website for recommendations.

Legal

There are several legal issues to consider when starting a business. These include the type of business entity, protection from personal liability, trademarks, and protection of intellectual property.

Administrative

Organization of your new business, business licenses, and tax considerations are some of the administrative issues that must be addressed.

Relationships

Joint ventures and affiliate programs are two examples of relationships you can establish with other companies. Relationships like these can help diversify the ways potential customers can learn about your business. This can also be a way to diversify revenues as your business grows.

Customer Research

There should be ongoing efforts to research the behavior of your customers. Continually learn about your customers' wants and needs to better attract them to your offerings.

Opportunity Cost

You only have so much time in a day. You only have so much bandwidth to start and grow your business. You can't do it all, and everything you do has an opportunity cost. Doing one thing means you must delay or forgo doing other things. Focus on your Vision and Mission to make the right choices for you.

Remember that "No" is a complete sentence. Learn to say no.

Sharpen Your Skills

You'll become extremely busy when you start your business. Even so, you must continue to sharpen your skills.

Learn on your own. Get a coach. Follow mentors. Join a Mastermind group. Attend live events. Sharpen the skills you need to better serve your customers.

Be Authentic

Don't get lost in your business. Your customers want the real you. Starting your business will be a transformative experience; just don't let it transform you into someone you're not.

Test Everything

You won't have all the answers. You'll be surprised how your customers react. Customers may show no interest in something you think is great, and they may love things that don't appeal to you.

Consider your business to be a laboratory for testing ideas. Don't pre-judge what will work. Instead, make a hypothesis and test it. Double down your efforts where customers are responding positively. Give up on areas where customers are negative or indifferent.

Things that worked yesterday may no longer be effective. Be open to change as needed.

Scale Back Your Lifestyle

Everyone starts their business in a different financial situation. Some have lots of capital to invest in their business, while others may only be able to invest "sweat equity." No matter the situation, you may want to consider scaling back your lifestyle.

A new business takes a while to develop. "Runway" is the term used to describe the amount of time the business can meet its obligations with cash on hand.

Scaling back your lifestyle gives you a longer personal runway for your business to become viable. You may find numerous expenses that could be eliminated without a serious impact on your quality of life.

I've recently extended my personal runway by eliminating several expenses that weren't absolutely necessary. I especially addressed expenses that also demanded time and energy.

Starting a business, you're about to become very busy!

Just Start

Finally, just start.

Tomorrow can't be better than today if you don't start. You can't serve your customers better until you start serving them. You can't take advantage of the Slight Edge until you start doing the next best thing.

In this chapter, we addressed critical issues related to being of service to your customers. You learned a simple framework to evaluate these issues as they come up.

You then learned the importance of customer-focused issues. These issues must be the focus of your attention because they are the source of your best learning and require your leadership.

Finally, I introduced several other potential business issues to consider.

You're now ready to get to work starting your business.

The next step is your 90-Day Action Plan.

Time to get started!

CHAPTER 9 – STEP 5: YOUR 90-DAY ACTION PLAN

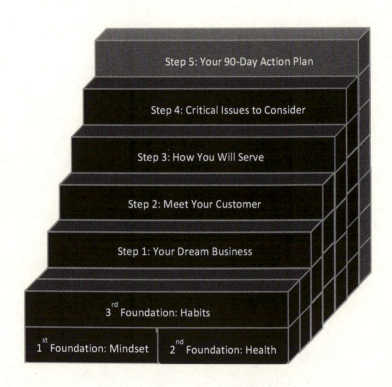

It's GO time.

You've come a long way. You now know the 3 Foundations of Success to start your business:

1. Mindset

2. Health

3. Habits

Then we covered the first four steps to starting your business:

1. Your Dream Business

2. Meet Your Customer

3. How You Will Serve

4. Critical Issues to Consider

Step 5, the final step, is to create your 90-Day Action Plan.

In this chapter, I'll share how to prepare for and structure your Action Plan. You will learn how to create a plan you can commit to following that will build momentum for your business.

I'll include recommendations on specific things to do and when to do them based on the foundations and steps we've covered thus far.

Your 90-Day Action Plan will be your marching orders as you start your new business.

Let's get started.

THE CASE FOR A 90-DAY ACTION PLAN

Consider this quote by Benjamin Franklin:

"By failing to prepare, you are preparing to fail."

I like the even tighter version: Fail to plan. Plan to fail.

It's so true, especially when starting a new business. Creating something out of nothing is hard work!

A 90-Day Action Plan is a time-tested tool. It captures everything you need to do during your first twelve weeks. It tracks your progress along the way, and helps you move toward your goal of starting your business.

As you build and follow your plan, you'll begin to feel a tremendous sense of accomplishment. Your plan will spur you to keep moving forward toward your dreams to make them a reality.

Preliminaries

Check my book resource page for links to 90-Day
Action Plan templates to download and follow.

I followed a 90-Day Action Plan to bring this book to
life. Before I started, I just had ideas swirling around
my head. My plan told me what I needed to do each
week to stay on track.

Make an appointment with your doctor the first action.
You need to know where you stand medically; starting
a business is physically and mentally challenging.

BUILDING YOUR PLAN

A plan is a series of goals, plus how and when you are
going to achieve them. From Entrepreneur On Fire's
John Lee Dumas I learned the acronym S.M.A.R.T. for
goals:

- Specific
- Measurable
- Actionable
- Relevant
- Timely

Your plan needs an overall goal for the end of the 90 days or twelve weeks. Decide what you can achieve.

Let's use this book as an example. My 90-day goal was to have the Kindle edition of this book available on Amazon.com.

This goal was specific. After 90 days the book was either available or it wasn't.

This goal was measurable. It could either be purchased on Amazon.com at that time or not.

This goal was actionable. Within 90 days, I had to write the book and do everything necessary to put it in the Kindle store. I knew the steps it would take to get it done.

This goal was relevant. My Mission is to inspire and support people over 50 who want to start their own business. This book is relevant to my Mission.

And finally, this goal was timely. I only gave myself 90 days to achieve this goal.

Make sure your goals are SMART.

Make sure your plan reflects the commitments you can actually make. I personally recommend "stretch" goals; goals that require dedicated effort to achieve within the time frame.

You can decide how much detail to put in your plan. I recommend dividing the 90-Day Action Plan into 12 consecutive weekly plans. Each week would have its own set of smaller goals and specific actions for that week.

You could even add greater detail to your plan by specifying daily goals and actions. Choose a comfortable level of detail. Choose the level of detail YOU need to meet each goal within its time frame.

Let's return to the example of this book. My 90-day goal was to have the book available on the Kindle store. I needed shorter term goals to make this happen. For example, the first draft needed to be written by week 6. This shorter term goal required its own set of smaller goals and specific tasks. All the way down to daily goals of writing at least 2 hours. It was all in my plan.

Additional Plan Recommendations

Document your plan. Put it down on paper. Your plan becomes real when you can hold it in your hands. Your milestones are real when you read them.

Also keep in mind that your plan is a living document. You will have great ideas along the way. Have a method to collect them. Don't just depend on your memory. Keep a notebook handy. Use your phone. Use an app like Evernote. Dictate your ideas. Draw or collect images. Whatever works for you.

You must prepare for good ideas. They will seem to appear by magic. Here's the method I use:

1. Plant the seed – Do research, talk with others, and think about the issue. This mix may be all you need.

2. Let go – Stop the research, stop thinking about the issue, and hand it off to your subconscious.

3. Wait, and be ready – Your subconscious is your wisdom. Give it time to work for you. When the ideas appear, be ready to collect them.

e. This is not magic. Good ideas are the meeting tion and inspiration.

Include the 3 Foundations

Make sure your plan includes goals and actions to address the three foundations. Make Mindset a habit. Make Health a habit. Put them explicitly in your plan. Make sure your plan reflects using the Slight Edge to get better each day in Mindset and Health.

I firmly believe that it is critical to build a Success Mindset. In the process of starting your dream business, there will be good times and there will be bad times. With a Success Mindset, you'll understand that hardships are an inevitable part of the process. You'll be prepared to face them and not give up. A Success Mindset gives you the mental and emotional strength to persevere. I recommend you include goals and actions at the start of your plan that build strong Mindset habits. Review Chapter 2.

Include Health habits in your plan too. Starting a business is a marathon; you must be healthy to succeed. Put physical activity, nutrition, and sleep goals into your plan. Review Chapter 3.

I highly recommend that your plan include a goal of developing your own version of a Daily Practice. Nearly every successful person has such a habit. A solid Daily Practice builds momentum for achieving all

147

your goals each day. For more on this, review Chapter 4.

You will find these Foundation habits will lead to a better life and will make achieving your business goals much easier. I sure did.

Creating your Action Plan and then following it builds a valuable habit too.

You should make a goal of completing at least the first two Steps in your 90-Day Action Plan. Give yourself plenty of time for each of these Steps.

Step 1: Your Dream Business. This should be fun and enlightening, but give yourself a few weeks to complete it. It takes a while for your passions and interests to reveal themselves, and you want to allow plenty of time to evaluate. Review Chapter 5 for more details.

Step 2: Meet Your Customer. Creating your Customer Avatar should also be a goal for the 90-Day Action Plan, because it will bring focus to every future goal and action in your business. Review Chapter 6.

Of course completing Steps 3 and 4 would also be great goals for the first 90 days, but I'll leave it up to you to plan for however much you feel comfortable with.

Document your plan. Don't just keep it in your head. Put it down on paper. Print it out. Sign it like a contract. Keep it handy. Do whatever you need to make it REAL for you.

Find others to hold you accountable to your plan. Tell others about your goals. A spouse or other family member could work. A friend or colleague could also work. An accountability partner or coach is even better.

Show them your plan. Let them know your goals and actions. Meet with them regularly. I recommend meeting at least once per week.

My website, **TheMaturEntrepreneur.com**, is a place for entrepreneurs over 50 like you. Share your story there. Share your progress. I built it for YOU!

Now that you know how to create your first 90-Day Action Plan for your dream business, read on for a few final words of encouragement before you get to work.

CONCLUSION – THE NEXT STEP IS YOURS

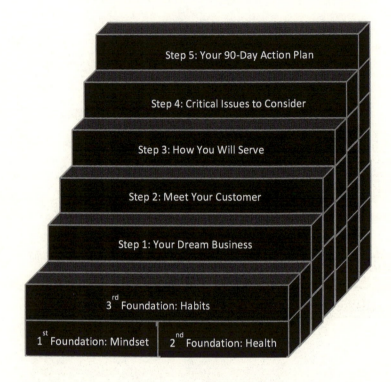

"The best way to predict the future is to create it."
– Abraham Lincoln

It's time for YOU to create your future.

It's time for you to start YOUR business.

You've come this far. You chose this book for a reason.

You're still concerned about the future. You know job security is a myth. You're worried about your retirement.

You're still interested in creating wealth. You want to control your destiny. You want to leave a legacy.

So what's different now?

You've read this book. You see there's a way.

You've learned the importance of a Success Mindset. You've learned that anything is possible. Age is no barrier. (I'd even argue that it's an advantage!)

You're ready to take 100% responsibility for your life.

You understand that Health is critical. Over 50 can be the new 30 if you stay active, eat well, and sleep well. Take care of yourself.

Good Habits make everything possible. You see the power of the Slight Edge. Doing the next best thing day after day leads to powerful positive change.

You see the power of having a Daily Practice to set the tone for success.

These are your Foundations for Success.

You also know the steps you need to take.

Step 1 is Your Dream Business. Open your imagination. Consider all possibilities. Uncover your passions. You offer a unique and valuable combination of passion and experience. In the Connected Economy, your passion can be your business.

In Step 2, you discovered your ideal customer, your Customer Avatar. Make your business about your customer and you will find success.

Steps 3 and 4 stress how you will serve your customers and learn from them as you go.

Focus on your WHY. Create Vision and Mission Statements and let them guide you.

Finally, in Step 5 you built your first 90-Day Action Plan to put all the Foundations and Steps in motion. You set SMART goals and outlined the weekly actions necessary to achieve them.

You are not the only person over 50 doing this.

More and more people over 50 are starting businesses, and they're seeing a higher success rate than their younger peers.

Follow the best practices in this book to increase your odds of success.

Management expert Jim Rohn said, *"Success is something you attract by the person you become."*

Become the owner of your dream business.

Start YOUR journey.

Take that first step.

I'm rooting for you.

Over 50? Start YOUR Business!

ABOUT THE AUTHOR

Brian D. Jones has a Mission to inspire and support people over 50 who want to start their own business. He enjoyed corporate success for over 10 years as an engineering project leader and management consultant. Since 1995, he has been a stay-at-home dad and home-based independent consultant. Brian graduated *magna cum laude* from Drake University in 1980 with a BA in Mathematics and Spanish. He was elected to *Phi Beta Kappa*. He earned a Master's degree from the Stanford School of Engineering. Brian also received his MBA from the Stanford Graduate School of Business. His website is www.TheMaturEntrepreneur.com.

Don't sleep on leaving a review!

Thank you for choosing my book! I really appreciate your feedback, and love hearing what you have to say.

Reviews are critical for first-time authors.

Please leave me a helpful REVIEW on Amazon.

Thanks so much!!
~ Brian (and Muggsy)

Made in the USA
Lexington, KY
25 August 2017